ICKY WORLD

WE NEED MUD!

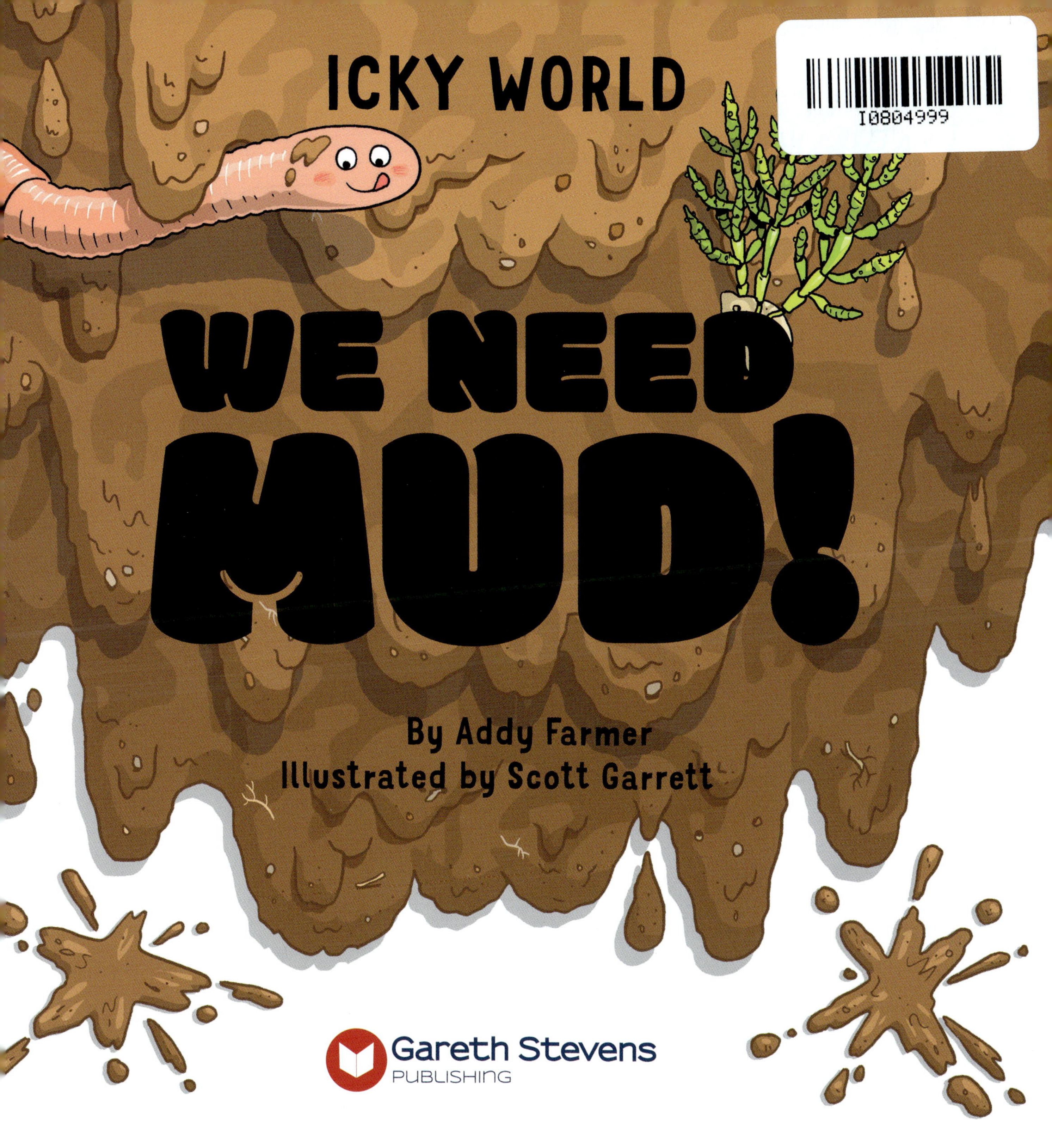

By Addy Farmer
Illustrated by Scott Garrett

Gareth Stevens
PUBLISHING

Please visit our website, www.garethstevens.com. For a free color catalog of all our high-quality books, call toll free 1-800-542-2595 or fax 1-877-542-2596.

Cataloging-in-Publication Data
Names: Farmer, Addy. | Garrett, Scott.
Title: We need mud! / Addy Farmer, illustrated by Scott Garrett.
Description: Buffalo, NY : Gareth Stevens Publishing, 2026. | Series: Icky world | Includes glossary and index.
Identifiers: ISBN 9781482472974 (pbk.) | ISBN 9781482472981 (library bound) | ISBN 9781482472998 (ebook)
Subjects: LCSH: Mud--Juvenile literature. | Soil ecology--Juvenile literature.
Classification: LCC QE471.2 F376 2026 | DDC 553.6.1 --dc23

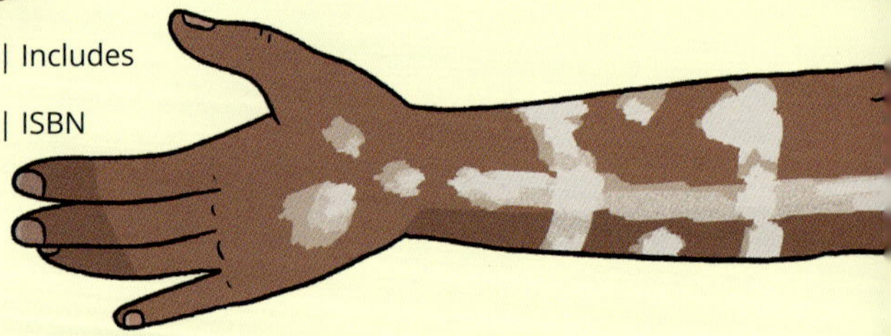

Published in 2026 by
Gareth Stevens Publishing
2544 Clinton St.
Buffalo, NY 14224

Series Editor: Grace Glendinning
Series Designer: Peter Scoulding

Printed in the United States of America

CPSIA compliance information: Batch #CSGS26: For further information contact Gareth Stevens at 1-800-542-2595.

CONTENTS

MUD: What on EARTH is it?

**Mud! Sludge, slush, ooze, mire, muck.
There are so many words for mud!
But what is it?**

Mud is a mixture of different types of soil and liquid. Soil is anything that is made of minerals, organic matter, living organisms, water, and air. Mud is everywhere–from the Australian Outback to Antarctica.

Mud is essential for **gardeners, farmers, animals,** and creative **mud-pie-makers**!

Mud on the seashore is made of **silt**.

Silt is tiny bits of sand and other materials carried by the water to the land. This mud oozes between your toes.

Watch your step! Silt is home to lots of mud-loving, marine creatures, such as **lugworms**, **cockles**, and **snails**.

Mud made from **clay** lies at the bottom of lakes and rivers, or in layers underground.

Clay mud can be any color from white to orange-red and it is very useful for making pottery or bricks.

Mudstone is a soft rock made from mud. It takes 200 million years to form.

Mud is amazing!

In the beginning ... there was MUD!

So where did all this mud come from?

When objects in space collided billions of years ago, they formed mud balls.

Many, many mud balls

The mud balls took different forms, from dwarf-planet-sized mud balls, to baby asteroids, to the meteorite that could land in your swimming pool!

These alien mud balls are like time capsules from the beginning of the solar system. By investigating them, we know how the planets formed and what they were made from, including our planet, Earth.

Mud shaped our world!

On a very young planet Earth, nearly 5 billion years ago, rivers were straight and flowed on bare rock. Any mud that formed–from the water mixing with dust as the rocks wore away–ran straight into the oceans.

As plant life began to grow on Earth, 500 million years ago, mud could grip onto its roots on the river's edge.

All the new plant growth and mud buildup made rivers twist and turn, and change the way the land looked.

Muddy Mars

Scientists also believe that there was once mud and water on Mars. There are tens of thousands of dead mud volcanoes on Mars, which may even have life hidden deep inside.

Volcanic mud on Earth, too, may have been the source of all life on our planet!

How does your garden grow?

Most of the world's plants grow out of icky mud, from tiny bumblebee orchids to giant redwood trees.

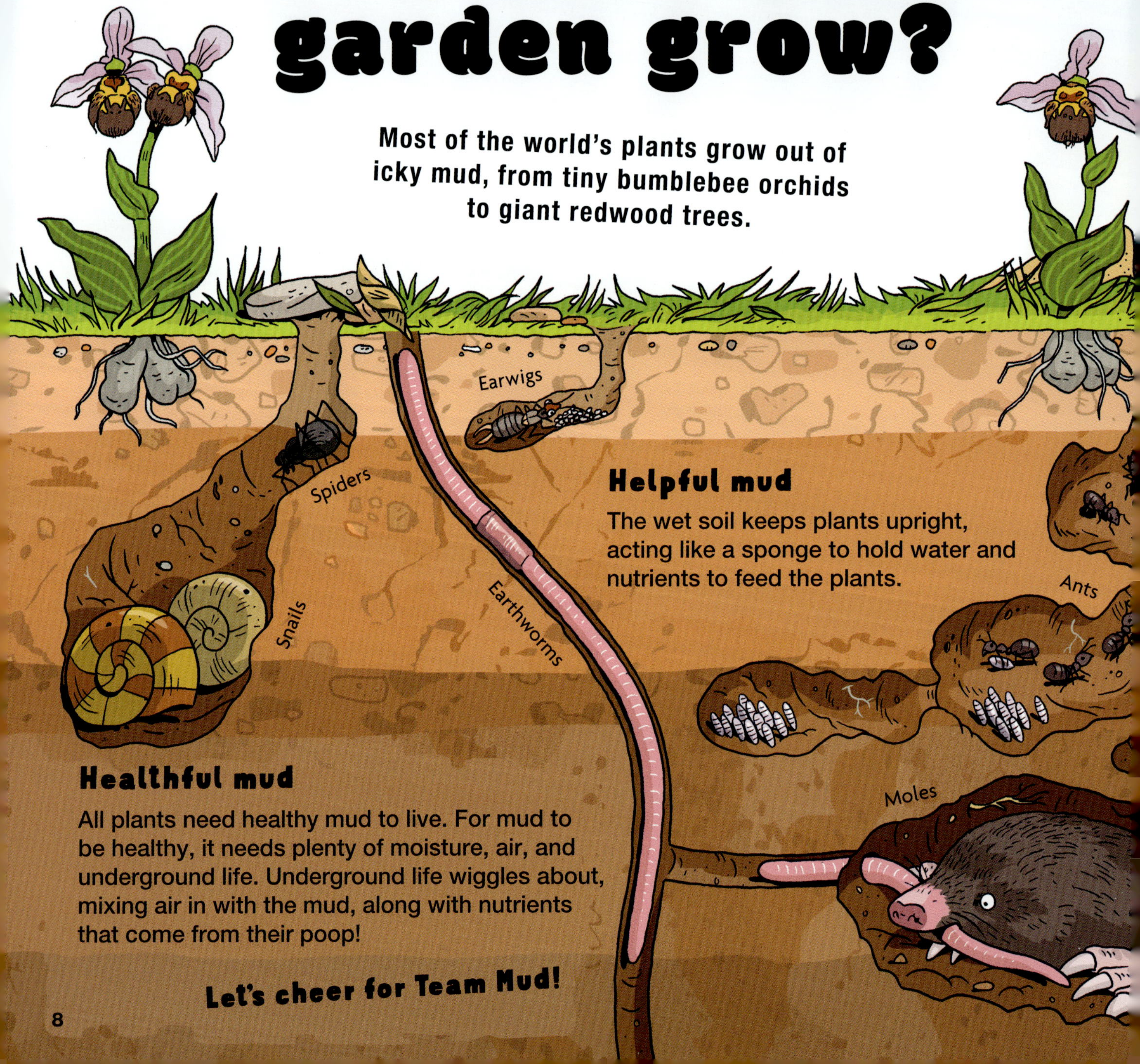

Helpful mud

The wet soil keeps plants upright, acting like a sponge to hold water and nutrients to feed the plants.

Healthful mud

All plants need healthy mud to live. For mud to be healthy, it needs plenty of moisture, air, and underground life. Underground life wiggles about, mixing air in with the mud, along with nutrients that come from their poop!

Let's cheer for Team Mud!

There are many different types of muddy soil:

Some plants, such as pine trees and lavender, grow well in **sandy soil**. It is light and well-drained.

Silty soil has medium-sized particles, which are easily squished down. This makes it dense and difficult to dig, plant, and pull weeds from!

Clay soil is heavy and full of nutrients and water. Plants such as Brussels sprouts have roots that like to be held firmly in clay.

If you dig up mud and find lots of white, stony bits, that's a **chalky soil**. This soil dries out quickly. But Mediterranean herbs, such as sage, like it.

Loamy soil is a mixture of sand, silt, and clay, and is very good for growing all types of plants and flowers–a gardener's favorite!

Peaty soil: see pages 10 and 11 for a special look at this fascinating type of muddy soil.

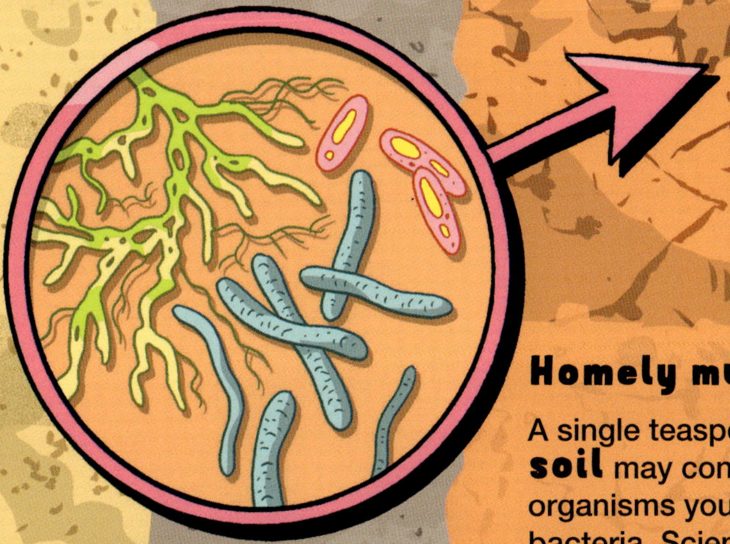

Homely mud

A single teaspoon of **garden soil** may contain thousands of organisms you can't see, such as bacteria. Scientists have worked out that at least one-quarter of all species on planet Earth live in soils.

Icky PEAT!

Peat is a type of rich mud that is very important for people, wildlife, and the planet.

Peat is formed in bogs from decaying marsh plants. Over thousands of years, this decaying organic matter builds up and becomes thick, muddy peat.

Amazing peat

Take a walk on peat and you will notice that it is squishy underfoot. This is because peat holds water like a sponge. About 10 percent of our planet's fresh water is stored in muddy peat (see page 25 for details on how peat helps our climate too).

In the past, peatlands have been nearly destroyed as peat was harvested for fuel and fertilizer. Today, many people work to preserve peatlands to help animals, plants, and the planet thrive.

These spongy peat bogs also slow down the flow of rainfall, helping to prevent flooding.

Peatland life

The plant and animal species found in peatland mud around the world are unique and varied.

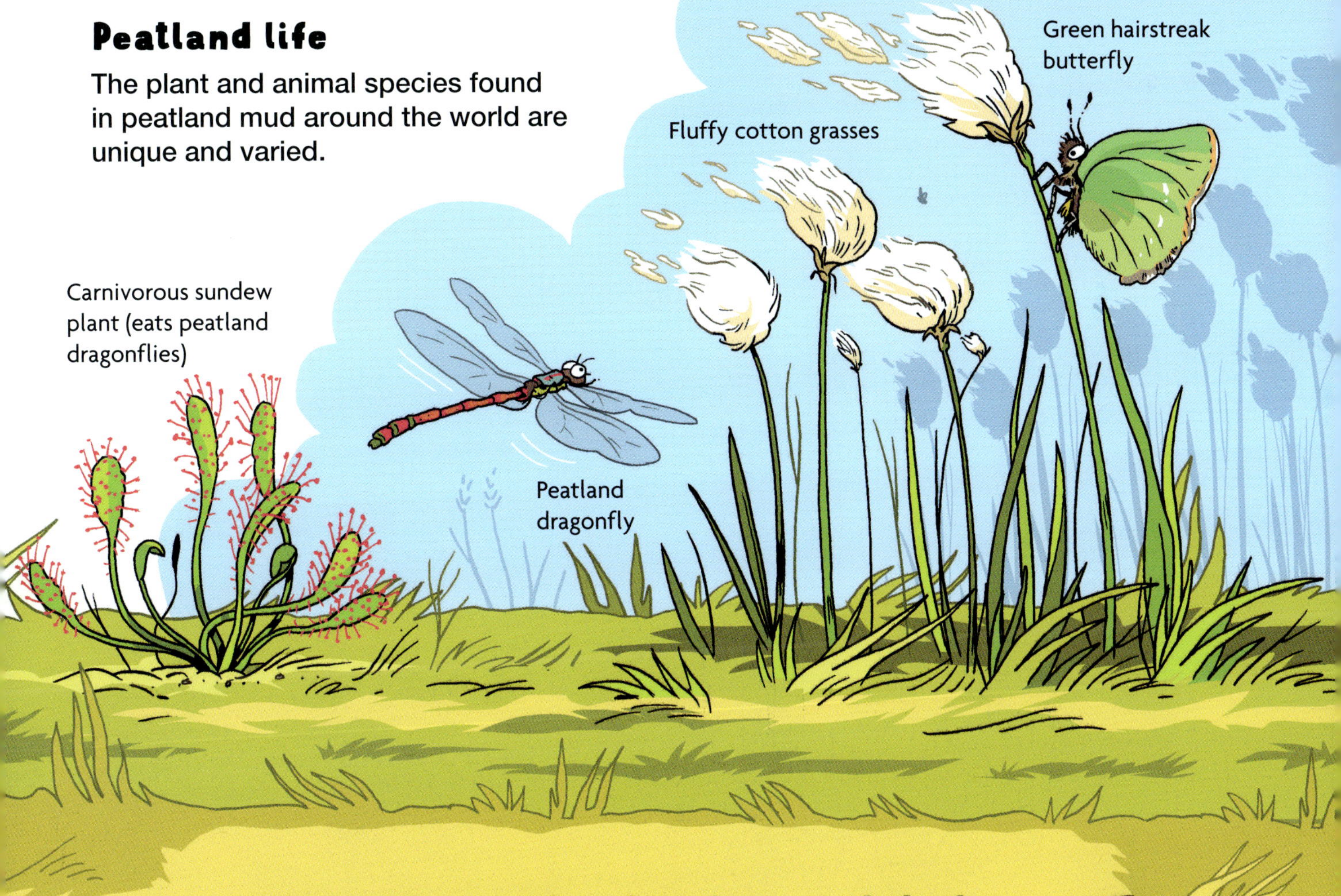

Birds, such as the **curlew**, **lapwing**, and **skylark**, nest on the peaty ground, where they can feed bugs to their young.

Muddy

Wallowing animals love to play in the mud.

In the heat, **hippopotamuses** bathe in mud to stay cool. Mud sticks to their bodies and keeps them cool longer than a dip in cold water. Bliss!

Elephants love mud-wallowing. Whole families use mud to cool down and get rid of pesky insects from their skin. The mud also acts as a sunscreen.

Peccaries are piglike animals from the Peruvian rainforests. Just like pigs on farms, peccaries love a cooling, skin-protecting wallow in a muddy hollow.

beasts

Mud can be a nursery, a home, or even a trap!

Mud dauber wasps build pipe-shaped mud nests for their eggs.

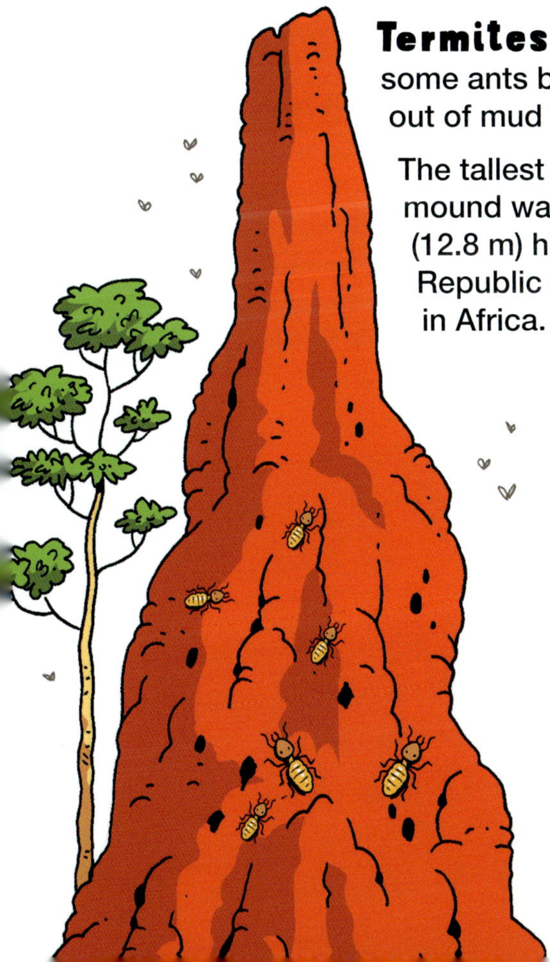

Termites and some ants build mounds out of mud to live in.

The tallest known termite mound was almost 42 feet (12.8 m) high, found in the Republic of Congo, in Africa.

One type of clever **dolphin** has been spotted using mud to make a sort of fishing net!

Amazing mud burrows

All sorts of animals burrow in the icky mud. It makes a wonderful home!

The **giant burrowing frog** from Australia spends nearly all its life hidden inside its riverbank burrow. It has thick, muscular arms and non-webbed feet for digging out its muddy home.

The **tiger salamander** is the largest land salamander in the world. Like any amphibian, it needs to live near water to keep its delicate skin moist. Its muddy home is often a hole in the soft earth.

Moles have an extra thumb on each forelimb that helps them dig in the muddy earth. The star-faced mole can find prey in the mud and eat it in just 0.23 seconds–the fastest of any mammal.

Burrowing crayfish and **fiddler crabs** are amazing mud architects!

As they dig out their muddy burrows, they form tall **"mud chimneys"** that harden and protect them from predators.

And we can't forget the **mudskipper**! This is a fish that can pull itself along on land with its fins, breathing by using tanks of water it holds in its gills.

As if that's not fascinating enough, the mudskipper builds its burrow by sucking up mud and spitting it out with a

SQUIRT!

Icky ecosystems

Mud is found in all of Earth's watery places, where it plays an important part in keeping those ecosystems healthy.

Mud under the surface

Mud on the seabed is a key part of all ocean ecosystems.

Mud-burrowing animals churn up the mud as they make their homes, pushing air into the seabed, and mixing in different nutrients and minerals.

This delicious, nutritious, muddy environment attracts lots of sea life.

Down at the bottom of the sea, the slimy, green **mud volcano worm** lives in total darkness. It burrows through the mud and can create mounds up to 3.2 feet (1 m) high.

Mud on the edge

Mudflats, mangroves, and salt marshes are other icky ecosystems where mud is vital. They are found where rivers meet the sea.

Waterfowl and wading birds love mud, and they usually have wide wings, long legs, and specially shaped beaks and feet to feed in the mud without sinking.

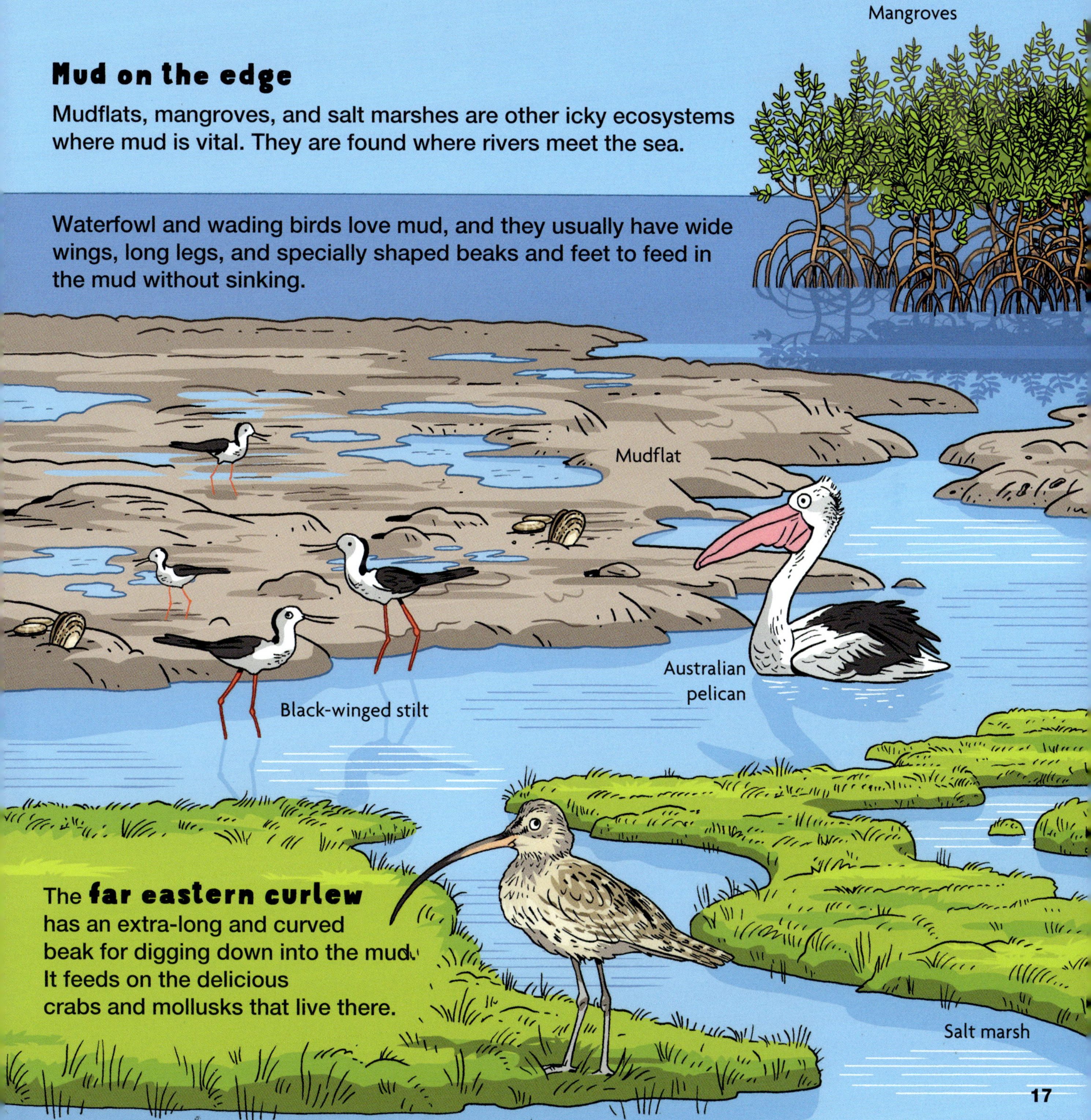

The **far eastern curlew** has an extra-long and curved beak for digging down into the mud. It feeds on the delicious crabs and mollusks that live there.

Muddy buildings

Humans have used mud to construct buildings since ancient times. Why? There is a lot of it around, and it is dirt cheap!

Even today, one-third of the Earth's population uses mud to build their houses.

Early Egyptians used mud to create bricks and build houses. Outside, the sun was hot, but inside, the mudbrick houses stayed cool in the day and warm at night. These muddy houses were also fireproof and stayed free of pesky termites.

The ancient walled city of **Shibham in Yemen** is known as the oldest mudbrick city in the world. Some of the buildings are almost 100 feet (30 m) high. They're often called the first skyscrapers!

The magnificent **mud mosque of Mali** is one of the largest buildings made entirely of mud. It can hold 3,000 worshippers.

Cob houses have been built out of mud for over 10,000 years. But there are no bricks here! People just mix up mud, water, and straw (cob), usually with their feet. Then the cob is formed into a wall.

Mudbricks to the rescue

As mud is a highly sustainable material when used properly, mudbrick-building is one way to help fight climate change.

Mud art

Mud is a key ingredient for creating art in every country around the world!

Muddy inspiration

The natural colors of mud have inspired artists for millennia. Stunning examples of this muddy beauty are the mud "paint pots" of Yellowstone National Park, with their bright colors and interesting shapes.

Clay mud is also very flexible. It can be molded into all sorts of shapes, from everyday pottery to extraordinary, decorated sculptures.

Pottery has other names. such as ceramics, porcelain, or even china–because the earliest pottery came from China.

But it all starts as mud!

Chinese pottery

Greek pottery

British pottery

Mud army

In 1974, farmers in China made one of the most incredible mud art finds: the Terracotta Army. This is a vast clay army built over 2,200 years ago, which was created to protect the emperor in his afterlife.

Mud instruments

Mud can make music too! All kinds of musical instruments can be made from clay, such as ocarinas, flutes, and even didgeridoos.

The xun is a musical instrument from China that has been in use for about 7,000 years.

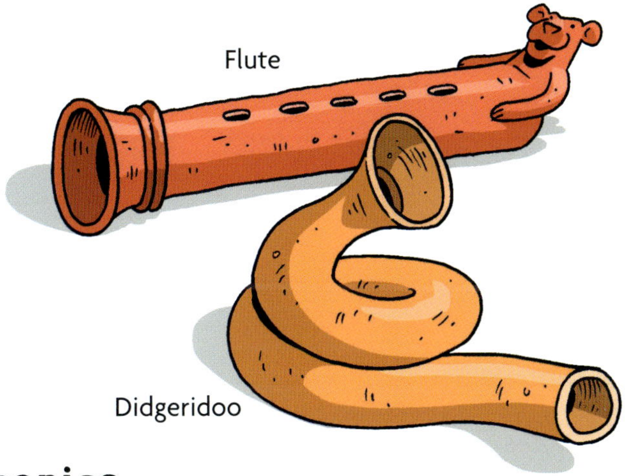

Mud in ceremonies

Some people even *become* art by decorating their bodies with colored clay mud. For example, some Aboriginal peoples in Australia do this on important occasions.

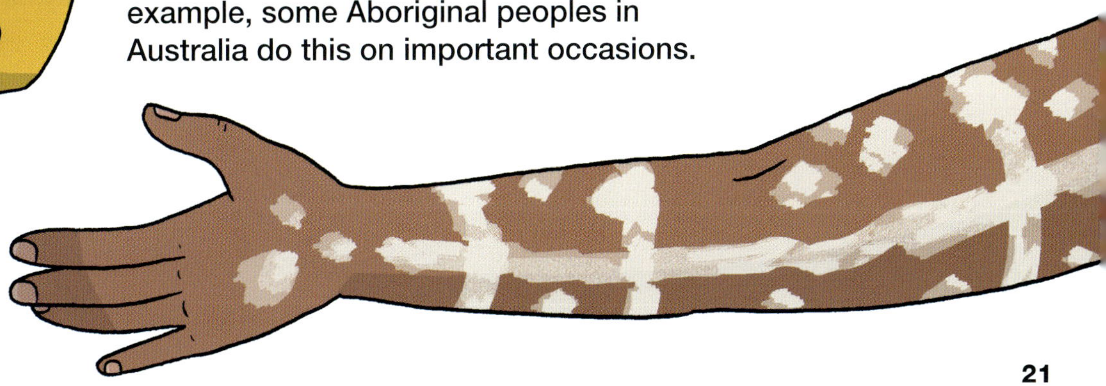

Muddy history

Mud helps to preserve evidence of our planet's past. It surrounds buried objects, shielding them from decay.

Paleontologists are scientists who look for fossils in prehistoric mud. Fossils help us understand what life was like millions of years ago.

About 250 million years ago, an ichthyosaur died.

It floated to the bottom of the sea. It was buried in the mud.

The mud hardened and became rock. Paleontologists then discover it preserved by the mud.

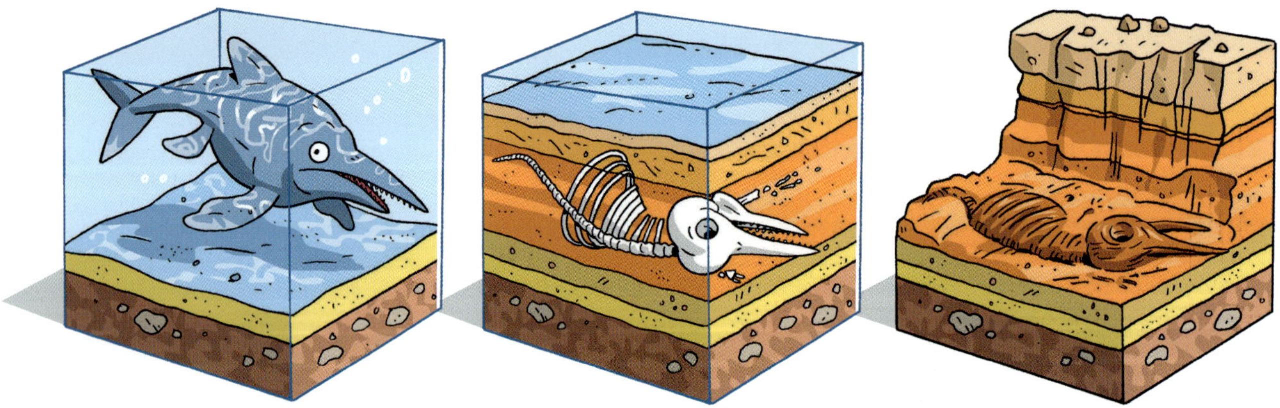

Archaeologists are scientists who dig in ancient mud to uncover buried objects from the more recent past. Using special tools, they test samples of the ancient mud surrounding each find to help them figure out:

- the time period of the objects preserved in the mud
- which plants grew in the area and which animals grazed there
- what the local people ate, how they lived, and how they died.

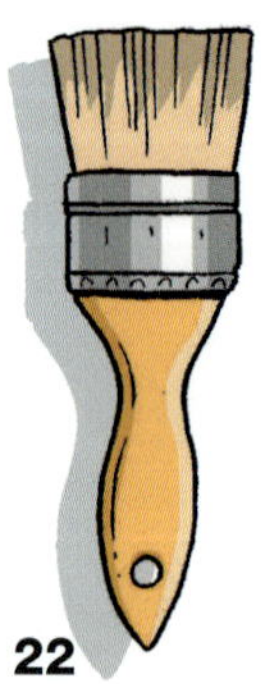

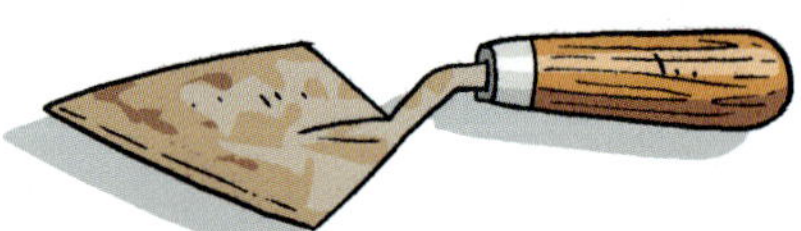

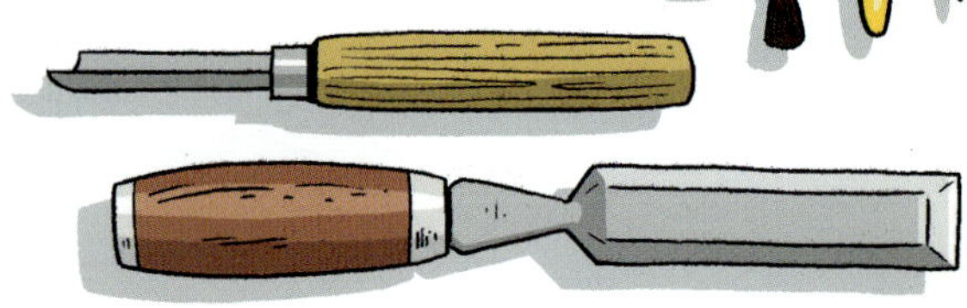

Just like paleontologists and archaeologists, **mudlarkers** are fascinated with history found in the mud. They have fun hunting through the mud on riverbanks (with special permission).

Mudlarkers find all sorts of lost objects, from woolly mammoth teeth to Roman hairpins made of bone! This hobby is popular in the UK.

Bog bodies

Tollund Man is a famous 2,000-year-old "bog body." The peaty mud mummified him. His skin, organs, and even his clothing were preserved.

Thanks to mud, archaeologists learned a lot about Tollund Man and the people of his time, even that his last meal was porridge and fish!

Muddy problems

If we don't look after our mud, there will be big consequences for our planet.

Our mud is already being damaged by humans in lots of ways.

Mud mistakes

Sometimes farmers grow huge amounts of just one type of plant to feed lots of people or animals. This can make the soil weak and unhealthy. No plants will grow properly in the field after a while.

Chemical pollution from factories and farming kills off the millions of organisms and animals that work together to keep mud healthy.

The roots of plants and trees help to hold muddy soil together and prevent erosion. When forests are cut down to clear land for other uses, it can lead to flooding or even disastrous mudslides.

Mud out of balance

All our different muddy soils, but especially peat, are very important for storing carbon. This gas can be held safely underground by the mud, helping to keep our climate in balance.

On the other hand, *unhealthy* mud releases carbon dioxide, which is one cause of climate change. Then, as the planet heats, the mud heats and dries up, and releases even more gases into the atmosphere!

Not to mention that drying-up mud means habitat damage for countless animals. If a muddy water hole dries up, where will the elephants go to wallow?

Stick with mud ...

We should all think carefully about and celebrate our muddy environments.

When you stand on healthy mud, you are surrounded by a huge variety of plants, animals, and billions of hardworking underground organisms. We can look at, smell, and touch this beautiful biodiversity*.

Playing in the mud

Some people think that playing in the mud as children helps us develop lots of good microbes inside our bodies and keeps us healthy (called a healthy microbiome).

In Finland they are even bringing forest soil into city homes to try and introduce good microbes to children. (Don't try this at home unless you have permission!)

*As long as we always wash our hands well afterwards!

... and save our world!

There's always more to learn about mud!

Mud rescue

Around the world, people are starting to restore the world's delicate ecosystems, such as ancient mudflats and saltmarshes, to boost biodiversity further and trap more carbon!

Mud: our friend

By working *with* nature, farmers and other businesses can keep our soils healthy far into the future. A healthy soil means a reliable source of food for animals and people.

If we take care of our mud, we can keep our planet a place of wonder, health, and inspiration for all.

Get your hands dirty!

Here are some practical tips for keeping the mud you see healthy.

Do not disturb

If you go out into nature, bring your trash home. Leave only your footprints in the mud!

Also, stick to the footpaths. Straying off pathways can erode soil across habitats and disturb or even kill wildlife.

Improve biodiversity

Transform a small patch of a garden or park near you. Let it go wild! All you have to do is leave it alone, and then look out for the birds and insects who move in.

You could even add a few wildflower seeds to make sure a variety of plants are growing in your soil.

Peat activism

Perhaps you can encourage your family or school to buy peat-free composts for their gardens so the peatlands can remain undisturbed?

Glossary

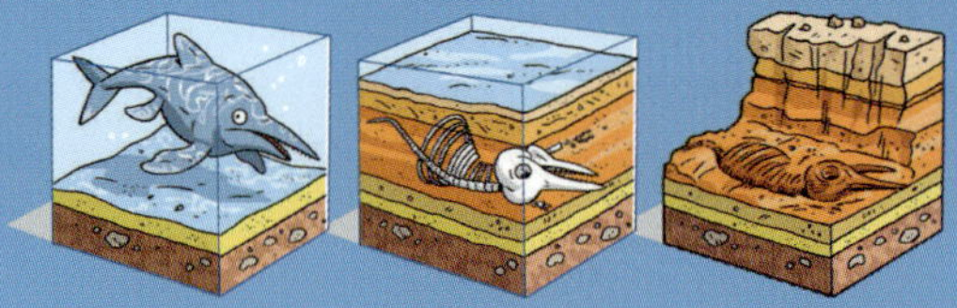

Amphibians – cold-blooded vertebrates (vertebrates have backbones) that don't have scales. They live part of their lives in water and part on land.

Archaeologists – people who dig underground to uncover buried artifacts from the past.

Asteroid – a small rocky object that orbits the sun. When a small piece of an asteroid burns up upon entering Earth's atmosphere, it's called a meteor. When a piece of a meteor lands on Earth, it is called a meteorite.

Biodiversity – all the variety of life, whether that's plants, animals, fungi or microorganisms, as well as the ecosystems they form and the habitats in which they live.

Carbon dioxide – a gas found in the air, which plants absorb during photosynthesis (how they make their own food).

Climate change – the process of our planet heating up and our world weather changing. This is due to many reasons, including carbon dioxide escaping into the atmosphere. For example, carbon is released when humans clear land of plants so that they can build or mine.

Cob – a mixture of clay, mud, and straw used to make walls.

Ecosystem – all the organisms living in a certain area and how they interact with that environment to form a natural community.

Fertilizer – a material added to soil or land to make it better able to support life.

Fossils – the remains or traces of plants and animals that lived a long time ago.

Fossil fuels – the natural fuels made from fossilized plants and animals, such as coal and oil.

Microbes – the tiny living microorganisms you cannot see with the naked eye, for example bacteria and viruses.

Microbiome – lots of good microbes inside our bodies that keep us healthy.

Mud volcanoes – holes in the Earth's crust where hot water and natural gases mix and mud erupts instead of lava.

Paleontologists – scientists who look for and study fossils in ancient mud.

Peat – a type of soil made from dead plants that have not completely rotted. It takes thousands of years for a large area of peat to form.

Sustainable (or "green") building – a building that, in its design or construction, has as little impact as possible on the environment.

Further info

Find out more about the icky bits of nature!

Books:
Disgustring Science Jobs, by Mary E Bleckwehl (Black Rabbit Books, 2023)

1,000 Amazing Gross Facts, By Stevie Derrick, et al.
(Dorling Kindersley Limited, 2023)

21 Things to Do with a Mud Pie: An Outdoor Activity Book, by Jane Wilsher
(Ivy Kids Eco, 2024)

Websites:

www.rspb.org.uk/our-work/casework/cases/wallasea-island
Find out about estuaries and mudflats wildlife in the United Kingdom, including the inspiring work being done at Wallasea Island mudflats

spaceplace.nasa.gov
Learn more about the origins of the universe.

INDEX